DUTCHMAN *and* THE SLAVE

William Morrow and Company · New York · 1964

two plays by LeRoi Jones

DUTCHMAN

and

THE SLAVE

Published simultaneously in the
Dominion of Canada by George J. McLeod Limited, Toronto.
Printed in the United States of America
Library of Congress Catalog Card Number 64-22207

• • • • • • • • • • • • • • • • •

For Thomas Everett Russ, American pioneer,
and Anna Cherry Brock Russ, his wife

DUTCHMAN

DUTCHMAN was first presented at The Cherry Lane Theatre, New York City on March 24, 1964

Original Cast

Jennifer West   Robert Hooks

Produced by Theater 1964
(Richard Barr, Clinton Wilder, Edward Albee)
Directed by Edward Parone

Characters

CLAY, twenty-year-old Negro

LULA, thirty-year-old white woman

RIDERS OF COACH, white and black

YOUNG NEGRO

CONDUCTOR

In the flying underbelly of the city. Steaming hot, and summer on top, outside. Underground. The subway heaped in modern myth.

Opening scene is a man sitting in a subway seat, holding a magazine but looking vacantly just above its wilting pages. Occasionally he looks blankly toward the window on his right. Dim lights and darkness whistling by against the glass. (Or paste the lights, as admitted props, right on the subway windows. Have them move, even dim and flicker. But give the sense of speed. Also stations, whether the train is stopped or the glitter and activity of these stations merely flashes by the windows.)

The man is sitting alone. That is, only his seat is visible, though the rest of the car is outfitted as a complete subway car. But only his seat is shown. There might be, for a time, as the play begins, a loud scream of the actual train. And it can recur throughout the play, or continue on a lower key once the dialogue starts.

The train slows after a time, pulling to a brief stop at one of the stations. The man looks idly up, until he sees a woman's face staring at him through the window; when it realizes that the man has noticed the face, it begins very premeditatedly to smile. The man smiles too, for a moment, without a trace of self-consciousness. Almost an instinctive though undesirable response. Then a kind of awkwardness or embarrassment sets in, and the man makes to look away, is further embarrassed, so he brings back his eyes to where the face was, but by now the train is moving again, and the face would seem to be left behind by the way the man turns his head to look back through the other windows at the slowly fading platform. He smiles then; more comfortably confident, hoping perhaps that his memory of this brief encounter will be pleasant. And then he is idle again.

Scene I

Train roars. Lights flash outside the windows.

LULA enters from the rear of the car in bright, skimpy summer clothes and sandals. She carries a net bag full of paper books, fruit, and other anonymous articles. She is wearing sunglasses, which she pushes up on her forehead from time to time. LULA is a tall, slender, beautiful woman with long red hair hanging straight down her back, wearing only loud lipstick in somebody's good taste. She is eating an apple, very daintily. Coming down the car toward CLAY.

She stops beside CLAY's seat and hangs languidly from the strap, still managing to eat the apple. It is apparent that she is going to sit in the seat next to CLAY, and that she is only waiting for him to notice her before she sits.

CLAY sits as before, looking just beyond his magazine, now and again pulling the magazine slowly back and forth in front of his face in a hopeless effort to fan himself. Then he sees the woman hanging there beside him and he looks up into her face, smiling quizzically.

LULA. Hello.   *Adam eatening Eve of the subway!*

CLAY. Uh, hi're you?

→ Man is made from clay # clay is moldable!

LULA. I'm going to sit down. . . . O.K.?

CLAY. Sure.

LULA.
  [*Swings down onto the seat, pushing her legs straight out as if she is very weary*]
Oooof! Too much weight.

CLAY. Ha, doesn't look like much to me.
  [*Leaning back against the window, a little surprised and maybe stiff*]

LULA. It's so anyway.
  [*And she moves her toes in the sandals, then pulls her right leg up on the left knee, better to inspect the bottoms of the sandals and the back of her heel. She appears for a second not to notice that* CLAY *is sitting next to her or that she has spoken to him just a second before.* CLAY *looks at the magazine, then out the black window. As he does this, she turns very quickly toward him*]
Weren't you staring at me through the window?

CLAY.
  [*Wheeling around and very much stiffened*]
What?

LULA. Weren't you staring at me through the window? At the last stop?

CLAY. Staring at you? What do you mean?

LULA. Don't you know what staring means?

CLAY. I saw you through the window . . . if that's what

it means. I don't know if I was staring. Seems to me you were staring through the window at me.

LULA. I was. But only after I'd turned around and saw you staring through that window down in the vicinity of my ass and legs.

CLAY. Really?

LULA. Really. I guess you were just taking those idle pot-shots. Nothing else to do. Run your mind over people's flesh.

CLAY. Oh boy. Wow, now I admit I was looking in your direction. But the rest of that weight is yours.

LULA. I suppose.

CLAY. Staring through train windows is weird business. Much weirder than staring very sedately at abstract asses.

LULA. That's why I came looking through the window . . . so you'd have more than that to go on. I even smiled at you.

CLAY. That's right.

LULA. I even got into this train, going some other way than mine. Walked down the aisle . . . searching you out.

CLAY. Really? That's pretty funny.

LULA. That's pretty funny. . . . God, you're dull.

CLAY. Well, I'm sorry, lady, but I really wasn't prepared for party talk.

LULA. No, you're not. What are you prepared for?
[*Wrapping the apple core in a Kleenex and dropping it on the floor*]

CLAY.
[*Takes her conversation as pure sex talk. He turns to confront her squarely with this idea*]
I'm prepared for anything. How about you?

LULA.
[*Laughing loudly and cutting it off abruptly*]
What do you think you're doing?

CLAY. What?

LULA. You think I want to pick you up, get you to take me somewhere and screw me, huh?

CLAY. Is that the way I look?

LULA. You look like you been trying to grow a beard. That's exactly what you look like. You look like you live in New Jersey with your parents and are trying to grow a beard. That's what. You look like you've been reading Chinese poetry and drinking lukewarm sugarless tea.
[*Laughs, uncrossing and recrossing her legs*]
You look like death eating a soda cracker.

CLAY.

> [*Cocking his head from one side to the other, embarrassed
> and trying to make some comeback, but also intrigued by
> what the woman is saying . . . even the sharp city coarseness
> of her voice, which is still a kind of gentle sidewalk throb*]

Really? I look like all that?

LULA. Not all of it.

> [*She feints a seriousness to cover an actual somber tone*]

I lie a lot.

> [*Smiling*]

It helps me control the world.

CLAY.

> [*Relieved and laughing louder than the humor*]

Yeah, I bet.

LULA. But it's true, most of it, right? Jersey? Your bumpy
neck?

CLAY. How'd you know all that? Huh? Really, I mean
about Jersey . . . and even the beard. I met you before?
You know Warren Enright?

LULA. You tried to make it with your sister when you
were ten.

> [CLAY *leans back hard against the back of the seat, his eyes
> opening now, still trying to look amused*]

But I succeeded a few weeks ago.

> [*She starts to laugh again*]

CLAY. What're you talking about? Warren tell you that?
You're a friend of Georgia's?

LULA. I told you I lie. I don't know your sister. I don't know Warren Enright.

CLAY. You mean you're just picking these things out of the air?

LULA. Is Warren Enright a tall skinny black black boy with a phony English accent?

CLAY. I figured you knew him.

LULA. But I don't. I just figured you would know some-body like that.
    [*Laughs*]

CLAY. Yeah, yeah.

LULA. You're probably on your way to his house now.

CLAY. That's right.

LULA.
    [*Putting her hand on Clay's closest knee, drawing it from the knee up to the thigh's hinge, then removing it, watching his face very closely, and continuing to laugh, perhaps more gently than before*]
Dull, dull, dull. I bet you think I'm exciting.

CLAY. You're O.K.

LULA. Am I exciting you now?

CLAY. Right. That's not what's supposed to happen?

LULA. How do I know?
[*She returns her hand, without moving it, then takes it away
and plunges it in her bag to draw out an apple*]
You want this?

CLAY. Sure.

LULA.
[*She gets one out of the bag for herself*]
Eating apples together is always the first step. Or walking
up uninhabited Seventh Avenue in the twenties on week-
ends.
[*Bites and giggles, glancing at Clay and speaking in loose sing-
song*]
Can get you involved . . . boy! Get us involved. Um-huh.
[*Mock seriousness*]
Would you like to get involved with me, Mister Man?

CLAY.
[*Trying to be as flippant as Lula, whacking happily at the
apple*]
Sure. Why not? A beautiful woman like you. Huh, I'd be
a fool not to.

LULA. And I bet you're sure you know what you're talking
about.
[*Taking him a little roughly by the wrist, so he cannot eat
the apple, then shaking the wrist*]
I bet you're sure of almost everything anybody ever asked
you about . . . right?
[*Shakes his wrist harder*]
Right?

CLAY. Yeah, right. . . . Wow, you're pretty strong, you know? Whatta you, a lady wrestler or something?

LULA. What's wrong with lady wrestlers? And don't answer because you never knew any. Huh.
[*Cynically*]
That's for sure. They don't have any lady wrestlers in that part of Jersey. That's for sure.

CLAY. Hey, you still haven't told me how you know so much about me.

LULA. I told you I didn't know anything about *you* . . . you're a well-known type.

CLAY. Really?

LULA. Or at least I know the type very well. And your skinny English friend too.

CLAY. Anonymously?

LULA.
[*Settles back in seat, single-mindedly finishing her apple and humming snatches of rhythm and blues song*]
What?

CLAY. Without knowing us specifically?

LULA. Oh boy.
[*Looking quickly at Clay*]
What a face. You know, you could be a handsome man.

CLAY. I can't argue with you.

LULA.
[*Vague, off-center response*]
What?

CLAY.
[*Raising his voice, thinking the train noise has drowned part of his sentence*]
I can't argue with you.

LULA. My hair is turning gray. A gray hair for each year and type I've come through.

CLAY. Why do you want to sound so old?

LULA. But it's always gentle when it starts.
[*Attention drifting*]
Hugged against tenements, day or night.

CLAY. What?

LULA.
[*Refocusing*]
Hey, why don't you take me to that party you're going to?

CLAY. You must be a friend of Warren's to know about the party.

LULA. Wouldn't you like to take me to the party?
[*Imitates clinging vine*]
Oh, come on, ask me to your party.

CLAY. Of course I'll ask you to come with me to the party. And I'll bet you're a friend of Warren's.

LULA. Why not be a friend of Warren's? Why not?
 [*Taking his arm*]
Have you asked me yet?

CLAY. How can I ask you when I don't know your name?

LULA. Are you talking to my name?

CLAY. What is it, a secret?

LULA. I'm Lena the Hyena.

CLAY. The famous woman poet?

LULA. Poetess! The same!

CLAY. Well, you know so much about me . . . what's my name?

LULA. Morris the Hyena.

CLAY. The famous woman poet?

LULA. The same.
 [*Laughing and going into her bag*]
You want another apple?

CLAY. Can't make it, lady. I only have to keep one doctor away a day.

LULA. I bet your name is . . . something like . . . uh, Gerald or Walter. Huh?

CLAY. God, no.

LULA. Lloyd, Norman? One of those hopeless colored names creeping out of New Jersey. Leonard? Gag. . . .

CLAY. Like Warren?

LULA. Definitely. Just exactly like Warren. Or Everett.

CLAY. Gag. . . .

LULA. Well, for sure, it's not Willie.

CLAY. It's Clay.

LULA. Clay? Really? Clay what?

CLAY. Take your pick. Jackson, Johnson, or Williams.

LULA. Oh, really? Good for you. But it's got to be Williams. You're too pretentious to be a Jackson or Johnson.

CLAY. Thass right.

LULA. But Clay's O.K.

CLAY. So's Lena.

LULA. It's Lula.

CLAY. Oh?

LULA. Lula the Hyena.

CLAY. Very good.

LULA.

    [*Starts laughing again*]

Now you say to me, "Lula, Lula, why don't you go to this party with me tonight?" It's your turn, and let those be your lines.

CLAY. Lula, why don't you go to this party with me tonight, Huh?

LULA. Say my name twice before you ask, and no huh's.

CLAY. Lula, Lula, why don't you go to this party with me tonight?

LULA. I'd like to go, Clay, but how can you ask me to go when you barely know me?

CLAY. That is strange, isn't it?

LULA. What kind of reaction is that? You're supposed to say, "Aw, come on, we'll get to know each other better at the party."

CLAY. That's pretty corny.

LULA. What are you into anyway?

[*Looking at him half sullenly but still amused*]
What thing are you playing at, Mister? Mister Clay Williams?

[*Grabs his thigh, up near the crotch*]
What are *you* thinking about?

CLAY. Watch it now, you're gonna excite me for real.

LULA.
[*Taking her hand away and throwing her apple core through the window*]
I bet.

[*She slumps in the seat and is heavily silent*]

CLAY. I thought you knew everything about me? What happened?

[LULA *looks at him, then looks slowly away, then over where the other aisle would be. Noise of the train. She reaches in her bag and pulls out one of the paper books. She puts it on her leg and thumbs the pages listlessly.* CLAY *cocks his head to see the title of the book. Noise of the train.* LULA *flips pages and her eyes drift. Both remain silent*]

Are you going to the party with me, Lula?

LULA.
[*Bored and not even looking*]
I don't even know you.

CLAY. You said you know my type.

LULA.
[*Strangely irritated*]
Don't get smart with me, Buster. I know you like the palm of my hand.

CLAY. The one you eat the apples with?

LULA. Yeh. And the one I open doors late Saturday evening with. That's my door. Up at the top of the stairs. Five flights. Above a lot of Italians and lying Americans. And scrape carrots with. Also . . .
  [*Looks at him*]
the same hand I unbutton my dress with, or let my skirt fall down. Same hand. Lover.

CLAY. Are you angry about anything? Did I say something wrong?

LULA. Everything you say is wrong.
  [*Mock smile*]
That's what makes you so attractive. Ha. In that funnybook jacket with all the buttons.
  [*More animate, taking hold of his jacket*]
What've you got that jacket and tie on in all this heat for? And why're you wearing a jacket and tie like that? Did your people ever burn witches or start revolutions over the price of tea? Boy, those narrow-shoulder clothes come from a tradition you ought to feel oppressed by. A three-button suit. What right do you have to be wearing a three-button suit and striped tie? Your grandfather was a slave, he didn't go to Harvard.

CLAY. My grandfather was a night watchman.

LULA. And you went to a colored college where everybody thought they were Averell Harriman.

CLAY. All except me.

LULA. And who did you think you were? Who do you think you are now?

CLAY.
   [*Laughs as if to make light of the whole trend of the conversation*]
Well, in college I thought I was Baudelaire. But I've slowed down since.

LULA. I bet you never once thought you were a black nigger.
   [*Mock serious, then she howls with laughter.* CLAY *is stunned but after initial reaction, he quickly tries to appreciate the humor.* LULA *almost shrieks*]
A black Baudelaire.

CLAY. That's right.

LULA. Boy, are you corny. I take back what I said before. Everything you say is not wrong. It's perfect. You should be on television. NEGRO'S BEGIN ON TV COMMER.

CLAY. You act like you're on television already.

LULA. That's because I'm an actress.

CLAY. I thought so.

LULA. Well, you're wrong. I'm no actress. I told you I always lie. I'm nothing, honey, and don't you ever forget it.
   [*Lighter*]
Although my mother was a Communist. The only person in my family ever to amount to anything.

CLAY. My mother was a Republican.

LULA. And your father voted for the man rather than the party.

CLAY. Right!

LULA. Yea for him. Yea, yea for him.

CLAY. Yea!

LULA. And yea for America where he is free to vote for the mediocrity of his choice! Yea!

CLAY. Yea!

LULA. And yea for both your parents who even though they differ about so crucial a matter as the body politic still forged a union of love and sacrifice that was destined to flower at the birth of the noble Clay . . . what's your middle name?

CLAY. Clay.

LULA. A union of love and sacrifice that was destined to flower at the birth of the noble Clay Clay Williams. Yea! And most of all yea yea for you, Clay Clay. The Black Baudelaire! Yes!
     [*And with knifelike cynicism*]
My Christ. My Christ.

CLAY. Thank you, ma'am.

LULA. May the people accept you as a ghost of the future.
And love you, that you might not kill them when you can.

CLAY. What?

HE CONCEALS HIS HATRED FOR WHITES

LULA. You're a murderer, Clay, and you know it.
[*Her voice darkening with significance*]
You know goddamn well what I mean.

CLAY. I do?

LULA. So we'll pretend the air is light and full of perfume.

CLAY.
[*Sniffing at her blouse*]
It is.

LULA. And we'll pretend the people cannot see you. That
is, the citizens. And that you are free of your own history.
And I am free of my history. We'll pretend that we are
both anonymous beauties smashing along through the city's
entrails.
[*She yells as loud as she can*]
GROOVE!

Black

LULA STRIPPES HIM DOWN SO THAT HE CAN IDEN. HIMSELF / A SEXUAL THEME / HIS ERECTION & JACKULA

AN AROUSING OF HIM & SEX ETC.

Scene II

Scene is the same as before, though now there are other seats visible in the car. And throughout the scene other people get on the subway. There are maybe one or two seated in the car as the scene opens, though neither CLAY *nor* LULA *notices them.* CLAY's *tie is open.* LULA *is hugging his arm.*

CLAY. The party!

LULA. I know it'll be something good. You can come in with me, looking casual and significant. I'll be strange, haughty, and silent, and walk with long slow strides.

CLAY. Right.

LULA. When you get drunk, pat me once, very lovingly on the flanks, and I'll look at you cryptically, licking my lips.

CLAY. It sounds like something we can do.

LULA. You'll go around talking to young men about your mind, and to old men about your plans. If you meet a very close friend who is also with someone like me, we can stand together, sipping our drinks and exchanging codes of lust. The atmosphere will be slithering in love and half-love and very open moral decision.

CLAY. Great. Great.

LULA. And everyone will pretend they don't know your name, and then . . .
  [*She pauses heavily*]
later, when they have to, they'll claim a friendship that denies your sterling character.

CLAY.
  [*Kissing her neck and fingers*]
And then what?

LULA. Then? Well, then we'll go down the street, late night, eating apples and winding very deliberately toward my house.

CLAY. Deliberately?

LULA. I mean, we'll look in all the shopwindows, and make fun of the queers. Maybe we'll meet a Jewish Buddhist and flatten his conceits over some very pretentious coffee.

CLAY. In honor of whose God?

LULA. Mine.

CLAY. Who is . . . ?

LULA. Me . . . and you?

CLAY. A corporate Godhead.

LULA. Exactly. Exactly.
[*Notices one of the other people entering*]

CLAY. Go on with the chronicle. Then what happens to us?

LULA.
[*A mild depression, but she still makes her description trium-
phant and increasingly direct*]
To my house, of course.

CLAY. Of course.

LULA. And up the narrow steps of the tenement.

CLAY. You live in a tenement?

LULA. Wouldn't live anywhere else. Reminds me specifically of my novel form of insanity.

CLAY. Up the tenement stairs.

LULA. And with my apple-eating hand I push open the door
and lead you, my tender big-eyed prey, into my . . . God,
what can I call it . . . into my hovel.

CLAY. Then what happens?

LULA. After the dancing and games, after the long drinks
and long walks, the real fun begins.

CLAY. Ah, the real fun.
>   [*Embarrassed, in spite of himself*]
Which is . . . ?

LULA.
>   [*Laughs at him*]
Real fun in the dark house. Hah! Real fun in the dark house,
high up above the street and the ignorant cowboys. I lead
you in, holding your wet hand gently in my hand . . .

CLAY. Which is not wet?

LULA. Which is dry as ashes.

CLAY. And cold?

LULA. Don't think you'll get out of your responsibility that
way. It's not cold at all. You Fascist! Into my dark living
room. Where we'll sit and talk endlessly, endlessly.

CLAY. About what?

LULA. About what? About your manhood, what do you
think? What do you think we've been talking about all this
time?

CLAY. Well, I didn't know it was that. That's for sure.
Every other thing in the world but that.
>   [*Notices another person entering, looks quickly, almost in-
>   voluntarily up and down the car, seeing the other people in
>   the car*]
Hey, I didn't even notice when those people got on.

LULA. Yeah, I know.

CLAY. Man, this subway is slow.

LULA. Yeah, I know.

CLAY. Well, go on. We were talking about my manhood.

LULA. We still are. All the time.

CLAY. We were in your living room.

LULA. My dark living room. Talking endlessly.

CLAY. About my manhood.

LULA. I'll make you a map of it. Just as soon as we get to my house.

CLAY. Well, that's great.

LULA. One of the things we do while we talk. And screw.

CLAY.
 [*Trying to make his smile broader and less shaky*]
We finally got there.

LULA. And you'll call my rooms black as a grave. You'll say, "This place is like Juliet's tomb."

CLAY.
 [*Laughs*]
I might.

LULA. I know. You've probably said it before.

CLAY. And is that all? The whole grand tour?

LULA. Not all. You'll say to me very close to my face, many, many times, you'll say, even whisper, that you love me.

CLAY. Maybe I will.

LULA. And you'll be lying.

CLAY. I wouldn't lie about something like that.

LULA. Hah. It's the only kind of thing you will lie about. Especially if you think it'll keep me alive.

CLAY. Keep you alive? I don't understand.

LULA.
   [*Bursting out laughing, but too shrilly*]
Don't understand? Well, don't look at me. It's the path I take, that's all. Where both feet take me when I set them down. One in front of the other.

CLAY. Morbid. Morbid. You sure you're not an actress? All that self-aggrandizement.

LULA. Well, I told you I wasn't an actress . . . but I also told you I lie all the time. Draw your own conclusions.

CLAY. Morbid. Morbid. You sure you're not an actress? All scribed? There's no more?

LULA. I've told you all I know. Or almost all.

CLAY. There's no funny parts?

LULA. I thought it was all funny.

CLAY. But you mean peculiar, not ha-ha.

LULA. You don't know what I mean.

CLAY. Well, tell me the almost part then. You said almost all. What else? I want the whole story.

LULA.

[*Searching aimlessly through her bag. She begins to talk breathlessly, with a light and silly tone*]

All stories are whole stories. All of 'em. Our whole story . . . nothing but change. How could things go on like that forever? Huh?

[*Slaps him on the shoulder, begins finding things in her bag, taking them out and throwing them over her shoulder into the aisle*]

Except I do go on as I do. Apples and long walks with deathless intelligent lovers. But you mix it up. Look out the window, all the time. Turning pages. Change change change. Till, shit, I don't know you. Wouldn't, for that matter. You're too serious. I bet you're even too serious to be psychoanalyzed. Like all those Jewish poets from Yonkers, who leave their mothers looking for other mothers, or others' mothers, on whose baggy tits they lay their fumbling heads. Their poems are always funny, and all about sex.

CLAY. They sound great. Like movies.

LULA. But you change.
[*Blankly*]
And things work on you till you hate them.
[*More people come into the train. They come closer to the couple, some of them not sitting, but swinging drearily on the straps, staring at the two with uncertain interest*]

CLAY. Wow. All these people, so suddenly. They must all come from the same place.

LULA. Right. That they do.

CLAY. Oh? You know about them too?

LULA. Oh yeah. About them more than I know about you. Do they frighten you?

CLAY. Frighten me? Why should they frighten me?

LULA. 'Cause you're an escaped nigger.

CLAY. Yeah?

LULA. 'Cause you crawled through the wire and made tracks to my side.

CLAY. Wire?

LULA. Don't they have wire around plantations?

CLAY. You must be Jewish. All you can think about is wire. Plantations didn't have any wire. Plantations were big open whitewashed places like heaven, and everybody on 'em was grooved to be there. Just strummin' and hummin' all day.

LULA. Yes, yes.

CLAY. And that's how the blues was born.

LULA. Yes, yes. And that's how the blues was born.
   [*Begins to make up a song that becomes quickly hysterical. As she sings she rises from her seat, still throwing things out of her bag into the aisle, beginning a rhythmical shudder and twistlike wiggle, which she continues up and down the aisle, bumping into many of the standing people and tripping over the feet of those sitting. Each time she runs into a person she lets out a very vicious piece of profanity, wiggling and stepping all the time*]
And that's how the blues was born. Yes. Yes. Son of a bitch, get out of the way. Yes. Quack. Yes. Yes. And that's how the blues was born. Ten little niggers sitting on a limb, but none of them ever looked like him.
   [*Points to* CLAY, *returns toward the seat, with her hands extended for him to rise and dance with her*]
And that's how blues was born. Yes. Come on, Clay. Let's do the nasty. Rub bellies. Rub bellies.

CLAY.
   [*Waves his hands to refuse. He is embarrassed, but determined to get a kick out of the proceedings*]
Hey, what was in those apples? Mirror, mirror on the wall, who's the fairest one of all? Snow White, baby, and don't you forget it.

LULA.
   [*Grabbing for his hands, which he draws away*]

Come on, Clay. Let's rub bellies on the train. The nasty. The nasty. Do the gritty grind, like your ol' rag-head mammy. Grind till you lose your mind. Shake it, shake it, shake it, shake it! OOOOweeee! Come on, Clay. Let's do the choo-choo train shuffle, the navel scratcher.

CLAY. Hey, you coming on like the lady who smoked up her grass skirt.

LULA.
  [*Becoming annoyed that he will not dance, and becoming more animated as if to embarrass him still further*]
Come on, Clay . . . let's do the thing. Uhh! Uhh! Clay! Clay! You middle-class black bastard. Forget your social-working mother for a few seconds and let's knock stomachs. Clay, you liver-lipped white man. You would-be Christian. You ain't no nigger, you're just a dirty white man. Get up, Clay. Dance with me, Clay.

CLAY. Lula! Sit down, now. Be cool.

LULA.
  [*Mocking him, in wild dance*]
Be cool. Be cool. That's all you know . . . shaking that wildroot cream-oil on your knotty head, jackets buttoning up to your chin, so full of white man's words. Christ. God. Get up and scream at these people. Like scream meaningless shit in these hopeless faces.
  [*She screams at people in train, still dancing*]
Red trains cough Jewish underwear for keeps! Expanding smells of silence. Gravy snot whistling like sea birds. Clay. Clay, you got to break out. Don't sit there dying the way they want you to die. Get up.

CLAY. Oh, sit the fuck down.
[*He moves to restrain her*]
Sit down, goddamn it.

LULA.
[*Twisting out of his reach*]
Screw yourself, Uncle Tom. Thomas Woolly-head.
[*Begins to dance a kind of jig, mocking Clay with loud forced humor*]
There is Uncle Tom . . . I mean, Uncle Thomas Woolly-Head. With old white matted mane. He hobbles on his wooden cane. Old Tom. Old Tom. Let the white man hump his ol' mama, and he jes' shuffle off in the woods and hide his gentle gray head. Ol' Thomas Woolly-Head.
[*Some of the other riders are laughing now. A drunk gets up and joins* LULA *in her dance, singing, as best he can, her* "*song.*" CLAY *gets up out of his seat and visibly scans the faces of the other riders*]

CLAY. Lula! Lula!
[*She is dancing and turning, still shouting as loud as she can. The drunk too is shouting, and waving his hands wildly*]
Lula . . . you dumb bitch. Why don't you stop it?
[*He rushes half stumbling from his seat, and grabs one of her flailing arms*]

LULA. Let me go! You black son of a bitch.
[*She struggles against him*]
Let me go! Help!
[CLAY *is dragging her towards her seat, and the drunk seeks to interfere. He grabs* CLAY *around the shoulders and begins wrestling with him.* CLAY *clubs the drunk to the floor without releasing* LULA, *who is still screaming.* CLAY *finally gets her to the seat and throws her into it*]

CLAY. Now you shut the hell up.
    [*Grabbing her shoulders*]
Just shut up. You don't know what you're talking about.
You don't know anything. So just keep your stupid mouth
closed.

LULA. You're afraid of white people. And your father was.
Uncle Tom Big Lip!

CLAY.
    [*Slaps her as hard as he can, across the mouth.* LULA's *head*
    bangs against the back of the seat. When she raises it again,
    CLAY *slaps her again*]
Now shut up and let me talk.
    [*He turns toward the other riders, some of whom are sitting*
    on the edge of their seats. The drunk is on one knee, rubbing
    his head, and singing softly the same song. He shuts up too
    when he sees CLAY *watching him. The others go back to news-*
    papers or stare out the windows]
Shit, you don't have any sense, Lula, nor feelings either. I
could murder you now. Such a tiny ugly throat. I could
squeeze it flat, and watch you turn blue, on a humble. For
dull kicks. And all these weak-faced ofays squatting around
here, staring over their papers at me. Murder them too.
Even if they expected it. That man there . . .
    [*Points to well-dressed man*]
I could rip that *Times* right out of his hand, as skinny and
middle-classed as I am, I could rip that paper out of his hand
and just as easily rip out his throat. It takes no great effort.
For what? To kill you soft idiots? You don't understand
anything but luxury.

LULA. You fool!

CLAY.

[*Pushing her against the seat*]

I'm not telling you again, Tallulah Bankhead! Luxury. In your face and your fingers. You telling me what I ought to do.

[*Sudden scream frightening the whole coach*]

Well, don't! Don't you tell me anything! If I'm a middle-class fake white man . . . let me be. And let me be in the way I want.

[*Through his teeth*]

I'll rip your lousy breasts off! Let me be who I feel like being. Uncle Tom. Thomas. Whoever. It's none of your business. You don't know anything except what's there for you to see. An act. Lies. Device. Not the pure heart, the pumping black heart. You don't ever know that. And I sit here, in this buttoned-up suit, to keep myself from cutting all your throats. I mean wantonly. You great liberated whore! You fuck some black man, and right away you're an expert on black people. What a lotta shit that is. The only thing you know is that you come if he bangs you hard enough. And that's all. The belly rub? You wanted to do the belly rub? Shit, you don't even know how. You don't know how. That ol' dipty-dip shit you do, rolling your ass like an elephant. That's not my kind of belly rub. Belly rub is not Queens. Belly rub is dark places, with big hats and overcoats held up with one arm. Belly rub hates you. Old bald-headed four-eyed ofays popping their fingers . . . and don't know yet what they're doing. They say, "I love Bessie Smith." And don't even understand that Bessie Smith is saying, "Kiss my ass, kiss my black unruly ass." Before love, suffering, desire, anything you can explain, she's say-

SHE GETS INTO HIS BLACK BRAIN FOR HE IS A FAKE LIKE A WHITE MIDDLE CLASS WHITE.

ing, and very plainly, "Kiss my black ass." And if you don't
know that, it's you that's doing the kissing.

Charlie Parker? Charlie Parker. All the hip white boys
scream for Bird. And Bird saying, "Up your ass, feeble-
minded ofay! Up your ass." And they sit there talking
about the tortured genius of Charlie Parker. Bird would've
played not a note of music if he just walked up to East
Sixty-seventh Street and killed the first ten white people he
saw. Not a note! And I'm the great would-be poet. Yes.
That's right! Poet. Some kind of bastard literature . . . all
it needs is a simple knife thrust. Just let me bleed you, you
loud whore, and one poem vanished. A whole people of
neurotics, struggling to keep from being sane. And the only
thing that would cure the neurosis would be your murder.
Simple as that. I mean if I murdered you, then other white
people would begin to understand me. You understand? No.
I guess not. If Bessie Smith had killed some white people she
wouldn't have needed that music. She could have talked
very straight and plain about the world. No metaphors. No
grunts. No wiggles in the dark of her soul. Just straight two
and two are four. Money. Power. Luxury. Like that. All of
them. Crazy niggers turning their backs on sanity. When
all it needs is that simple act. Murder. Just murder! Would
make us all sane.
   [*Suddenly weary*]
Ahhh. Shit. But who needs it? I'd rather be a fool. Insane.
Safe with my words, and no deaths, and clean, hard thoughts,
urging me to new conquests. My people's madness. Hah!
That's a laugh. My people. They don't need me to claim
them. They got legs and arms of their own. Personal in-

WHEN STRIPPED HE TURNS TO MURDER

sanities. Mirrors. They don't need all those words. They
don't need any defense. But listen, though, one more thing.
And you tell this to your father, who's probably the kind of
man who needs to know at once. So he can plan ahead. Tell
him not to preach so much rationalism and cold logic to
these niggers. Let them alone. Let them sing curses at you
in code and see your filth as simple lack of style. Don't
make the mistake, through some irresponsible surge of
Christian charity, of talking too much about the advantages
of Western rationalism, or the great intellectual legacy of
the white man, or maybe they'll begin to listen. And then,
maybe one day, you'll find they actually do understand exactly what you are talking about, all these fantasy people.
All these blues people. And on that day, as sure as shit, when
you really believe you can "accept" them into your fold, as
half-white trusties late of the subject peoples. With no more
blues, except the very old ones, and not a watermelon in
sight, the great missionary heart will have triumphed, and
all of those ex-coons will be stand-up Western men, with
eyes for clean hard useful lives, sober, pious and sane, and
they'll murder you. They'll murder you, and have very
rational explanations. Very much like your own. They'll
cut your throats, and drag you out to the edge of your
cities so the flesh can fall away from your bones, in sanitary
isolation.

LULA.

[*Her voice takes on a different, more businesslike quality*]
I've heard enough.

CLAY.

[*Reaching for his books*]

I bet you have. I guess I better collect my stuff and get off this train. Looks like we won't be acting out that little pageant you outlined before.

LULA. No. We won't. You're right about that, at least.
[*She turns to look quickly around the rest of the car*]
All right!
[*The others respond*]

CLAY.
[*Bending across the girl to retrieve his belongings*]
Sorry, baby, I don't think we could make it.
[*As he is bending over her, the girl brings up a small knife and plunges it into* CLAY's *chest. Twice. He slumps across her knees, his mouth working stupidly*]

LULA. Sorry is right.
[*Turning to the others in the car who have already gotten up from their seats*]
Sorry is the rightest thing you've said. Get this man off me! Hurry, now!
[*The others come and drag* CLAY's *body down the aisle*]
Open the door and throw his body out.
[*They throw him off*]
And all of you get off at the next stop.
[LULA *busies herself straightening her things. Getting every-thing in order. She takes out a notebook and makes a quick scribbling note. Drops it in her bag. The train apparently stops and all the others get off, leaving her alone in the coach.*

Very soon a young Negro of about twenty comes into the coach, with a couple of books under his arm. He sits a few seats in back of LULA. *When he is seated she turns and gives him a long slow look. He looks up from his book and drops the book on his lap. Then an old Negro conductor comes into*

White Liberals = who then serves as executioner

the car, doing a sort of restrained soft shoe, and half mumbling the words of some song. He looks at the young man, briefly, with a quick greeting]

CONDUCTOR. Hey, brother!

YOUNG MAN. Hey.

[*The conductor continues down the aisle with his little dance and the mumbled song.* LULA *turns to stare at him and follows his movements down the aisle. The conductor tips his hat when he reaches her seat, and continues out the car*]

Curtain

If man can not express himself, then he still remains a "boy."

Lula = in arousing Clay, also castrates him at the same time.

She is representative of the American woman.

Dutchman = Romantic or Gothic novel / Myth = "dealing in"

THE SLAVE

A Fable in a Prologue and Two Acts

THE SLAVE was first presented at the St. Mark's Playhouse, New York City, in December, 1964

Original Cast

GRACE   Nan Martin
WALKER   Al Freeman, Jr.
EASLEY   Jerome Raphel

Produced by Leo Garen and Stan Swerdlow in association with Gene Persson

Directed by Leo Garen
Designed by Larry Rivers

Characters

WALKER VESSELS, tall, thin Negro about forty.

GRACE, blonde woman about same age. Small, thin, beautiful.

BRADFORD EASLEY, tall, broad white man, with thinning hair, about forty-five.

The action takes place in a large living room, tastefully furnished the way an intelligent university professor and his wife would furnish it.

Room is dark at the beginning of the play, except for light from explosions, which continue, sometimes close, sometimes very far away, throughout both acts, and well after curtain of each act.

Hate expressed

Hatred permitt. enslaved the Black man.

Walker suffers from his hatred / the hate destroys

Black art is properganda according to L. Jones

Prologue

→ *is destroyed as well as destroying*

WALKER. *dressed like a old field slave at begin. & end of play*

[*Coming out dressed as an old field slave, balding, with white hair, and an old ragged vest. (Perhaps he is sitting, sleeping, initially-nodding and is awakened by faint cries, like a child's.) He comes to the center of the stage slowly, and very deliberately, puffing on a pipe, and seemingly uncertain of the reaction any audience will give his speech*]

Whatever the core of our lives. Whatever the deceit. We live where we are, and seek nothing but ourselves. We are liars, and we are murderers. We invent death for others. Stop their pulses publicly. Stone possible lovers with heavy worlds we think are ideas . . . and we know, even before these shapes are realized, that these worlds, these depths or heights we fly to smoothly, as in a dream, or slighter, when we stare dumbly into space, leaning our eyes just behind a last quick moving bird, then sometimes the place and twist of what we are will push and sting, and what the crust of our stance has become will ring in our ears and shatter that piece of our eyes that is never closed. An ignorance. A stupidity. A stupid longing not to know . . . which is au-

which shows that nothing was accomplished in blowing up the city

tomatically fulfilled. Automatically triumphs. Automatically makes us killers or foot-dragging celebrities at the core of any filth. And it is a deadly filth that passes as whatever thing we feel is too righteous to question, too deeply felt to deny.

[*Pause to relight pipe*]

I am much older than I look . . . or maybe much younger. Whatever I am or seem . . .

[*Significant pause*]

to you, then let that rest. But figure, still, that you might not be right. Figure, still, that you might be lying . . . to save yourself. Or myself's image, which might set you crawling like a thirsty dog, for the meanest of drying streams. The meanest of ideas.

[*Gentle, mocking laugh*]

Yeah. Ideas. Let that settle! Ideas. Where they form. Or whose they finally seem to be. Yours? The other's? Mine?

[*Shifts uneasily, pondering the last*]

No, no more. Not mine. I served my slow apprenticeship . . . and maybe came up lacking. Maybe. Ha. Who's to say, really? Huh? But figure, still, ideas are still in the world. They need judging. I mean, they don't come in that singular or wild, that whatever they are, just because they're beautiful and brilliant, just because they strike us full in the center of the heart. . . . My God!

[*Softer*]

My God, just because, and even this, believe me, even if, that is, just because they're *right* . . . doesn't mean anything. The very rightness stinks a lotta times. The very rightness.

[*Looks down and speaks softer and quicker*]

I am an old man. An old man.

[*Blankly*]

The waters and wars. Time's a dead thing really . . . and keeps nobody whole. An old man, full of filed rhythms. Terrific, eh? That I hoarded so much dignity? An old man full of great ideas. Let's say theories. As: Love is an instrument of knowledge. Oh, not my own. Not my own . . . is right. But listen now. . . . Brown is not brown except when used as an intimate description of personal phenomenological fields. As your brown is not my brown, et cetera, that is, we need, ahem, a meta-language. We need something not included here.

[*Spreads arms*]

Your ideas? An old man can't be expected to be right. If I'm old. If I really claim that embarrassment.

[*Saddens . . . brightens*]

A poem? Lastly, that, to distort my position? To divert you . . . in your hour of need. Before the thing goes on. Before you get your lousy chance. Discovering racially the funds of the universe. Discovering the last image of the thing. As the sky when the moon is broken. Or old, old blues people moaning in their sleep, singing, man, oh, nigger, nigger, you still here, as hard as nails, and takin' no shit from nobody. He say, yeah, yeah, he say yeah, yeah. He say, yeah, yeah . . . goin' down slow, man. Goin' down slow. He say . . . yeah, heh . . .

[*Running down, growing anxiously less articulate, more "field hand" sounding, blankly lyrical, shuffles slowly around, across the stage, as the lights dim and he enters the set proper and assumes the position he will have when the play starts . . . still moaning . . .*]

*Grace to Walker = you don't
know what the hell you
are doing.*

Act I

THE SCENE: *A light from an explosion lights the room
dimly for a second and the outline of a figure is seen half
sprawled on a couch. Every once in a while another blast
shows the figure in silhouette. He stands from time to time,
sits, walks nervously around the room examining books and
paintings. Finally, he climbs a flight of stairs, stays for a few
minutes, then returns. He sits smoking in the dark, until some
sound is heard outside the door. He rises quickly and takes a
position behind the door, a gun held out stiffly.* GRACE *and*
EASLEY *open the door, turn on the light, agitated and breathing heavily.* GRACE *quiet and weary.* EASLEY *talking in harsh
angry spurts.*

EASLEY. Son of a bitch. Those black son of a bitches. Why
don't they at least stop and have their goddamned dinners?
Goddamn son of a bitches. They're probably gonna keep
that horseshit up all goddamn night. Goddamnit. Goddamn it!

[*He takes off a white metal hat and slings it across the room.
It bangs loudly against the brick of the fireplace*]

GRACE. Brad! You're going to wake up the children!

EASLEY. Oh, Christ! . . . But if they don't wake up under all that blasting, I don't think that tin hat will do it.

[*He unbuttons his shirt, moves wearily across the room, still mumbling under his breath about the source of the explosions*]

Hey, Grace . . . you want a drink? That'll fix us up.

[*He moves to get the drink and spots* WALKER *leaning back against the wall, half smiling, also very weary, but still holding the gun, stomach high, and very stiffly.* EASLEY *freezes, staring at* WALKER's *face and then the gun, and then back to* WALKER's *face. He makes no sound. The two men stand confronting each other until* GRACE *turns and sees them*]

GRACE. Sure, I'll take a drink . . . one of the few real pleasures left in the Western world.

[*She turns and drops her helmet to the floor, staring unbelievingly*]

Ohh!

WALKER.

[*Looks over slowly at* GRACE *and waves as from a passing train. Then he looks back at* EASLEY; *the two men's eyes are locked in the same ugly intensity.* WALKER *beckons to* GRACE]

The blinds.

GRACE. Walker!

[*She gets the name out quietly, as if she is trying to hold so many other words in*]

Walker . . . the gun!

WALKER.

[*Half turning to look at her. He looks back at* EASLEY, *then lets the gun swing down easily toward the floor. He looks back at* GRACE, *and tries to smile*]

Hey, momma. How're you?

EASLEY.

[*At* WALKER, *and whatever else is raging in his own head*]
Son of a bitch!

GRACE. What're you doing here, Walker? What do you want?

WALKER.

[*Looking at* EASLEY *from time to time*]
Nothing. Not really. Just visiting.
[*Grins*]
I was in the neighborhood; thought I'd stop by and see how the other half lives.

GRACE. Isn't this dangerous?
[*She seems relieved by* WALKER's *relative good spirits and she begins to look for a cigarette.* EASLEY *has not yet moved. He is still staring at* WALKER]

WALKER. Oh, it's dangerous as a bitch. But don't you remember how heroic I am?

EASLEY.

[*Handing* GRACE *a cigarette, then waiting to light it*]
Well, what the hell do you want, hero?
[*Drawn out and challenging*]

WALKER.

[*With same challenge*]
Nothing you have, fellah, not one thing.

EASLEY. Oh?
[*Cynically*]

Is *that* why you and your noble black brothers are killing
what's left of this city?

[*Suddenly broken*]

I should say . . . what's left of this country . . . or world.

WALKER. Oh, fuck you

[*Hotly*]

fuck you . . . just fuck you, that's all. Just fuck you!

[*Keeps voice stiffly contained, but then it rises sharply*]

I mean really, just fuck you. Don't, goddamnit, don't tell
me about any goddamn killing of anything. If that's what's
happening. I mean if this shitty town is being flattened . . .
let it. It needs it.

GRACE. Walker, shut up, will you?

[*Furious from memory*]

I had enough of your twisted logic in my day . . . you
remember? I mean like your heroism. The same kind of
memory. Or Lie. Do you remember which? Huh?

[*Starting to weep*]

WALKER.

[*Starts to comfort her*]

Grace . . . look . . . there's probably nothing I can say
to make you understand me . . . now.

EASLEY.

[*Steps in front of* WALKER *as he moves toward* GRACE . . .
feigning a cold sophistication]

Uh. . . no, now come, Jefe, you're not going to make one
of those embrace the weeping ex-wife dramas, are you?

Well, once a bad poet always a bad poet . . . even in the disguise of a racist murderer!

WALKER.

[*Not quite humbled*]

Yeah.

[*Bends head, then he brings it up quickly, forcing the joke*]

Even disguised as a racist murderer . . . I remain a bad poet. Didn't St. Thomas say that? Once a bad poet always a bad poet . . . or was it Carl Sandburg, as some kind of confession?

EASLEY. You're not still writing . . . now, are you? I should think the political, now military estates would be sufficient. And you always used to speak of the Renaissance as an evil time.

[*Begins making two drinks*]

And now you're certainly the gaudiest example of Renaissance man I've heard of.

[*Finishes making drinks and brings one to* GRACE. WALKER *watches him and then as he starts to speak he walks to the cabinet, picks up the bottle, and empties a good deal of it*]

GRACE.

[*Looking toward* WALKER *even while* EASLEY *extends the drink toward her*]

Walker . . . you are still writing, aren't you?

WALKER. Oh, God, yes. Want to hear the first lines of my newest work?

[*Drinks, does a theatrical shiver*]

Uh, how's it go . . .? Oh, "Straddling each dolphin's back/ And steadied by a fin,/Those innocents relive their death,/ Their wounds open again."

GRACE.
    [*Staring at him closely*]
It's changed quite a bit.

WALKER. Yeah . . . it's changed to Yeats.
    [*Laughs very loudly*]
Yeah, Yeats. . . . Hey, professor, anthologist, lecturer, loyal opposition, et cetera, et cetera, didn't you recognize those words as being Yeats's? Goddamn, I mean if you didn't recognize them . . . who the hell would? I thought you knew all kinds of shit.

EASLEY.
    [*Calmly*]
I knew they were Yeats'.

WALKER.
    [*Tilting the bottle again quickly*]
Oh, yeah? What poem?

EASLEY. The second part of "News for the Delphic Oracle."

WALKER.
    [*Hurt*]
"News for the Delphic Oracle." Yeah. That's right.
    [*To* GRACE]
You know that, Grace? Your husband knows all about everything. The second part of "News for the Delphic Oracle."
    [*Rhetorically*]
Intolerable music falls. Nymphs and satyrs copulate in the foam.
    [*Tilts bottle again, some liquor splashes on the floor*]

EASLEY.

> [*Suddenly straightening and stopping close to* WALKER]

Look . . . LOOK! You arrogant maniac, if you get drunk or fall out here, so help me, I'll call the soldiers or some-body . . . and turn you over to them. I swear I'll do that.

GRACE. Brad!

WALKER. Yeah, yeah, I know. That's your job. A liberal education, and a long history of concern for minorities and charitable organizations can do that for you.

EASLEY.

> [*Almost taking hold of* WALKER's *clothes*]

No! I mean this, friend! Really! If I get the slightest advan-tage, some cracker soldier will be bayoneting you before the night is finished.

WALKER.

> [*Slaps* EASLEY *across the face with the back of his left hand, pulling the gun out with his right and shoving it as hard as he can against* EASLEY's *stomach.* EASLEY *slumps, and the cruelty in* WALKER's *face at this moment also frightens* GRACE]

"My country, 'tis of thee. Sweet land of liber-ty."

> [*Screams off key like drunken opera singer*]

Well, let's say liberty and ignorant vomiting faggot pro-fessors.

> [*To* GRACE]

Right, lady? Isn't that right? I mean you ought to know, 'cause you went out of your way to marry one.

> [*Turns to* GRACE *and she takes an involuntary step backward. And in a cracked ghostlike voice that he wants to be loud . . .*]

Huh? Huh? And then fed the thing my children.

> [*He reaches stiffly out and pushes her shoulder, intending it*

*to be strictly a burlesque, but there is quite a bit of force in
the gesture.* GRACE *falls back, just short of panic, but* WALKER
*hunches his shoulders and begins to jerk his finger at the ceil-
ing; one eye closed and one leg raised, jerking his finger ab-
surdly at the ceiling, as if to indicate something upstairs that
was to be kept secret*]

Ah, yes, the children . . .

[*Affecting an imprecise "Irish" accent*]

sure and they looked well enough . . .

[*Grins*]

and white enough, roosting in that kennel. Hah, I hope you
didn't tell Faggy, there, about those two lovely ladies.

[EASLEY *is kneeling on the floor holding his stomach and shaking his head*]

Ahh, no, lady, let's keep that strictly in the family. I mean
among those of us who screw.

[*He takes another long drink from the bottle, and "threatens"*
EASLEY'S *head in a kind of burlesque*]

For Lawrence, and all the cocksmen of my underprivileged
youth. When we used to chase that kind of frail little sissy-
punk down Raymond Boulevard and compromise his sister-
in-laws in the cloak room . . . It's so simple to work from
the bottom up. To always strike, and know, from the
blood's noise that you're right, and what you're doing is
right, and even *pretty*.

[*Suddenly more tender toward* GRACE]

I swear to you, Grace, I did come into the world pointed
in the right direction. Oh, shit, I learned so many words
for what I've wanted to say. They all come down on me
at once. But almost none of them are mine.

[*He straightens up, turning quickly toward the still kneeling*
EASLEY, *and slaps him as hard as he can across the face, send-
ing his head twisting around*]

Bastard! A poem for your mother!

GRACE.

> [*Lets out a short pleading cry*]

Ohh! Get away from him, Walker! Get away from him,

> [*Hysterically*]

you nigger murderer!

WALKER.

> [*Has started to tilt the bottle again, after he slaps* EASLEY, *and when* GRACE *shouts at him, he chokes on the liquor, spitting it out, and begins laughing with a kind of hysterical amusement*]

Oh! Ha, ha, ha . . . you mean . . . Wow!

> [*Trying to control laughter, but it is an extreme kind of release*]

No kidding? Grace, Gracie! Wow! I wonder how long you had that stored up.

GRACE.

> [*Crying now, going over to* EASLEY, *trying to help him up*]

Brad. Brad. Walker, why'd you come here? Why'd you come here? Brad?

WALKER.

> [*Still laughing and wobbling clumsily around*]

Nigger murderer? Wowee. Gracie, are you just repeating your faggot husband, or did you have that in you a long time? I mean . . . for all the years we were together? Hooo! Yeah.

> [*Mock seriously*]

Christ, it could get to be a weight after a time, huh? When you taught the little girls to pray . . . you'd have to whisper, "And God bless Mommy, and God bless Daddy, the nigger murderer." Wow, that's some weight.

GRACE. Shut up, Walker. Just shut up, and get out of here, away from us, please. I don't want to hear you . . . I don't need to hear you, again. Remember, I heard it all before, baby . . . you don't get me again.

> [*She is weeping and twisting her head, trying at the same time to fully revive* EASLEY, *who is still sitting on the floor with legs sprawled apart, both hands held to the pit of his stomach, his head nodding back and forth in pain*]

Why'd you come here . . . just to do this? Why don't you leave before you kill somebody?

> [*Trying to hold back a scream*]

Before you kill another white person?

WALKER.
> [*Sobering, but still forcing a cynical hilarity*]

Ah . . . the party line. Stop him before he kills another white person! Heh. Yeah. Yeah. And that's not such a bad idea, really. . . . I mean, after all, only you and your husband there are white in this house. Those two lovely little girls upstairs are niggers. You know, circa 1800, one drop makes you whole?

GRACE. Shut up, Walker!
> [*She leaps to her feet and rushes toward him*]

Shut your ugly head!
> [*He pushes her away*]

EASLEY.
> [*Raising his head and shouting as loud as he can manage*]

You're filth, boy. Just filth. Can you understand that anything and everything you do is stupid, filthy, or meaningless! Your inept formless poetry. Hah. Poetry? A flashy doggerel for inducing all those unfortunate troops of yours

to spill their blood in your behalf. But I guess that's something! Ritual drama, we used to call it at the university. The
poetry of ritual drama.

> [*Pulls himself up*]

And even that's giving that crap the benefit of the doubt.
Ritual filth would have been the right name for it.

WALKER. Ritual drama . . .

> [*Half musing*]

yeah, I remember seeing that phrase in an old review by
one of your queer academic friends. . . .

> [*Noticing* EASLEY *getting up*]

Oh well, look at him coming up by his bootstraps. I didn't
mean to hit you that hard, Professor Easley, sir . . . I just
don't know my own strent'.

> [*Laughs and finishes the bottle . . . starts as if he is going to
> throw it over his shoulder, then he places it very carefully on
> the table. He starts dancing around and whooping like an
> "Indian"*]

More! Bwana, me want more fire water!

EASLEY. As I said, Vessels, you're just filth. Pretentious filth.

WALKER.

> [*Dances around a bit more, then stops abruptly in front of
> EASLEY; so close they are almost touching. He speaks in a quiet
> menacing tone*]

The liquor, turkey. The liquor. No opinions right now.
Run off and get more liquor, *sabe?*

GRACE.

> [*Has stopped crying and managed to regain a cynical com-
> posure*]

I'll get it, Brad. Mr. Vessels is playing the mad scene from Native Son.

[*Turns to go*]

A second-rate Bigger Thomas.

WALKER.

[*Laughs*]

Yeah. But remember when I used to play a second-rate Othello? Oh, wow . . . you remember that, don't you, Professor No-Dick? You remember when I used to walk around wondering what that fair sister was thinking?

[*Hunches* EASLEY]

Oh, come on now, you remember that. . . . I was Othello . . . Grace there was Desdemona . . . and you were Iago . . .

[*Laughs*]

or at least between classes, you were Iago. Hey, who were you during classes? I forgot to find that out. Ha, the key to my downfall. I knew you were Iago between classes, when I saw you, but I never knew who you were during classes. Ah ah, that's the basis of an incredibly profound social axiom. I quote: . . . and you better write this down, Bradford, so you can pass it on to your hipper colleagues at the university . . .

[*Laughs*]

I mean if they ever rebuild the university. What was I saying to you, enemy? Oh yeah . . . the axiom. Oh . . .

GRACE.

[*Returning with a bottle*]

You still at it, huh, Bigger?

WALKER. Yeah, yeah . . .

[*Reaches for bottle*]

lemme see. I get it. . . . If a white man is Iago when you see him . . . uhh . . . chances are he's eviler when you don't.

[*Laughs*]

EASLEY. Yes, that was worthy of you.

WALKER. It *was* lousy, wasn't it?

GRACE. Look

[*Trying to be earnest*]

Walker, pour yourself a drink . . . as many drinks as you need . . . and then leave, will you? I don't see what you think you're accomplishing by hanging around us.

EASLEY. Yes . . . I was wondering who's taking care of your mighty army while you're here in the enemy camp? How can the black liberation movement spare its illustrious leader for such a long stretch?

WALKER.

[*Sits abruptly on couch and stretches both legs out, drinking big glass of bourbon. Begins speaking in pidgin "Japanese"*]

Oh, don't worry about that, doomed American dog. Ha. You see and hear those shells beating this town flat, don't you? In fact, we'll probably be here en masse in about a week. Why don't I just camp here and wait for my brothers to get here and liberate the whole place? Huh?

[*Laughs*]

GRACE. Walker, you're crazy!

EASLEY. I think he's got more sense than that.

WALKER.
> [*Starting to make up a song*]

Ohhh! I'll stay here and rape your wife . . . as I so often used to do . . . as I so often used . . .

GRACE. Your mind is gone, Walker . . . completely gone.
> [*She turns to go upstairs. A bright blast rocks the house and she falls against the wall*]

WALKER.
> [*Thrown forward to the floor, rises quickly to see how* GRACE *is*]

Hey, you all right, lady?

EASLEY. Grace!
> [*He has also been rocked, but he gets to* GRACE *first*]

Don't worry about my wife, Vessels. That's my business.

GRACE. I'm O.K., Brad. I was on my way upstairs to look in on the girls. It's a wonder they're not screaming now.

WALKER. They were fine when I looked in earlier. Sleeping very soundly.

EASLEY. You were upstairs?

WALKER.
> [*Returning to his seat, with another full glass*]

Of course I went upstairs, to see my children. In fact, I started to take them away with me, while you patriots were out.

[*Another close blast*]

But I thought I'd wait to say hello to the mommy and step-daddy.

EASLEY. You low bastard.
  [*Turning toward* WALKER *and looking at* GRACE *at the same time*]

GRACE. No . . . you're not telling the truth now, Walker.
  [*Voice quavering and rising*]
You came here just to say that. Just to see what your saying that would do to me.
  [*Turns away from him*]
You're a bad liar, Walker. As always . . . a very bad liar.

WALKER. You know I'm not lying. I want those children. You know that, Grace.

EASLEY. I know you're drunk!

GRACE. You're lying. You don't want those children. You just want to think you want them for the moment . . . to excite one of those obscure pathological instruments you've got growing in your head. Today, you want to feel like you want the girls. Just like you wanted to feel hurt and martyred by your misdirected cause, when you first drove us away.

WALKER. Drove you away? You knew what I was in to. You could have stayed. You said you wanted to pay whatever thing it cost to stay.

EASLEY. How can you lie like this, Vessels? Even I know you pushed Grace until she couldn't retain her sanity and stay with you in that madness. All the bigoted racist imbeciles you started to cultivate. Every white friend you had knows that story.

WALKER. You shut up. . . . I don't want to hear anything you've got to say.

GRACE. There are so many bulbs and screams shooting off inside you, Walker. So many lies you have to pump full of yourself. You're split so many ways . . . your feelings are cut up into skinny horrible strips . . . like umbrella struts . . . holding up whatever bizarre black cloth you're using this performance as your self's image. I don't even think you know who you are any more. No, I don't think you *ever* knew.

WALKER. I know what I can use.

GRACE. No, you never even found out who you were until you sold the last of your loves and emotions down the river . . . until you killed your last old friend . . . and found out *what* you were. My God, it must be hard being you, Walker Vessels. It must be a sick task keeping so many lying separate uglinesses together . . . and pretending they're something you've made and understand.

WALKER. What I can use, madam . . . what I can use. I move now trying to be certain of that.

EASLEY. You're talking strangely. What is this, the pragmatics of war? What are you saying . . . use? I thought you meant yourself to be a fantastic idealist? All those speeches and essays and poems . . . the rebirth of idealism. That the Western white man had forfeited the most impressive characteristic of his culture . . . the idealism of rational liberalism . . . and that only the black man in the West could restore that quality to Western culture, because he still understood the necessity for it. Et cetera, et cetera. Oh, look, I remember your horseshit theories, friend. I remember. And now the great black Western idealist is talking about use.

WALKER. Yeah, yeah. Now you can call me the hypocritical idealist nigger murderer. You see, what I want is more titles.

GRACE. And saying you want the children is another title . . . right? Every time you say it, one of those bulbs goes off in your head and you think you can focus on still another attribute, another beautiful quality in the total beautiful structure of the beautiful soul of Walker Vessels, sensitive Negro poet, savior of his people, deliverer of Western idealism . . . commander-in-chief of the forces of righteousness . . . Oh, God, et cetera, et cetera.

WALKER. Grace Locke Vessels Easley . . . whore of the middle classes.

EASLEY.
   [*Turning suddenly as if to offer combat*]
Go and fuck yourself.

GRACE. Yes, Walker, by all means . . . go and fuck yourself.

[*And softer*]

Yes, do anything . . . but don't drag my children into your scheme for martyrdom and immortality, or whatever else it is makes you like you are . . . just don't . . . don't even mention it.

EASLEY.

[*Moving to comfort her*]

Oh, don't get so worried, Grace . . . you know he just likes to hear himself talk . . . more than anything . . . he just wants to hear himself talk, so he can find out what he's supposed to have on his mind.

[*To* WALKER]

He knows there's no way in the world he could have those children. No way in the world.

WALKER.

[*Feigning casual matter-of-fact tone*]

Mr. Easley, Mrs. Easley, those girls' last name is Vessels. Whatever you think is all right. I mean I don't care what you think about me or what I'm doing . . . the whole mess. But those beautiful girls you have upstairs there are my daughters. They even look like me. I've loved them all their lives. Before this there was too much to do, so I left them with you.

[*Gets up, pours another drink*]

But now . . . things are changed. . . . I want them with me.

[*Sprawls on couch again*]

I want them with me very much.

GRACE. You're lying. Liar, you don't give a shit about those children. You're a liar if you say otherwise. You never never never cared at all for those children. My friend, you have never cared for anything in the world that I know of but what's in there behind your eyes. And God knows what ugliness that is . . . though there are thousands of people dead or homeless all over this country who begin to understand a little. And not just white people . . . you've killed so many of your own people too. It's a wonder they haven't killed you.

EASLEY.

[*Walks over to* WALKER]

Get up and get out of here! So help me . . . if you don't leave here now . . . I'll call the soldiers. They'd just love to find you.

[WALKER *doesn't move*]

Really, Vessels, I'll personally put a big hole in that foul liberation movement right now . . . I swear it.

[*He turns to go to the phone*]

WALKER.

[*At first as if he is good-natured*]

Hey, hey . . . Professor Easley, I've got this gun here, remember? Now don't do that . . . in fact if you take another step, I'll blow your goddamn head off. And I mean that, Brad, turn around and get back here in the center of the room.

GRACE.

[*Moves for the stairs*]

Ohhh!

WALKER. Hey, Grace, stop . . . you want me to shoot this fairy, or what? Come back here!

GRACE. I was only going to see about the kids.

WALKER. I'm their father . . . I'm thinking about their welfare, too. Just come back here. Both of you sit on this couch where I'm sitting, and I'll sit in that chair over there near the ice tray.

EASLEY. So now we get a taste of Vessels, the hoodlum.

WALKER. Uh, yeah. Another title, boss man. But just sit the fuck down for now.
[*Goes to the window. Looks at his watch*]
I got about an hour.

GRACE. Walker, what are you going to do?

WALKER. Do? Well, right now I'm going to have another drink.

EASLEY. You know what she means.

GRACE. You're not going to take the children, are you? You wouldn't just take them, would you? You wouldn't do that. You can't hate me so much that you'd do that.

WALKER. I don't hate you at all, Grace. I hated you when I wanted you. I haven't wanted you for a long time. But I do want those children.

GRACE. You're lying!

WALKER. No, I'm not lying . . . and I guess that's what's cutting you up . . . because you probably know I'm not lying, and you can't understand that. But I tell you now that I'm not lying, and that in spite of all the things I've done that have helped kill love in me, I still love those girls.

EASLEY. You mean, in spite of all the people you've killed.

WALKER. O.K., O.K., however you want it . . . however you want it, let it go at that. In spite of all the people I've killed. No, better, in spite of the fact that I, Walker Vessels, single-handedly, and with no other adviser except my own ego, promoted a bloody situation where white and black people are killing each other; despite the fact that I know that this is at best a war that will only change, ha, the complexion of tyranny . . .
  [Laughs sullenly]
in spite of the fact that I have killed for all times any creative impulse I will ever have by the depravity of my murderous philosophies . . . despite the fact that I am being killed in my head each day and by now have no soul or heart or warmth, even in my long killer fingers, despite the fact that I have no other thing in the universe that I love or trust, but myself . . . despite or in spite, the respite, my dears, my dears, hear me, O Olympus, O Mercury, God of thieves, O Damballah, chief of all the dead religions of pseudo-nigger patriots hoping to open big restaurants after de wah . . . har har . . . in spite, despite, the resistance in the large cities and the small towns, where we have taken, yes, dragged piles of darkies out of their beds and shot them

for being in Rheingold ads, despite the fact that all of my officers are ignorant motherfuckers who have never read any book in their lives, despite the fact that I would rather argue politics, or literature, or boxing, or anything, with you, dear Easley, with you . . .

[*Head slumps, weeping*]

despite all these things and in spite of all the drunken noises I'm making, despite . . . in spite of . . . I want those girls, very, very much. And I will take them out of here with me.

EASLEY. No, you won't . . . not if I can help it.

WALKER. Well, you can't help it.

GRACE.

[*Jumps up*]

What? Is no one to reason with you? Isn't there any way something can exist without you having the final judgment on it? Is the whole world yours . . . to deal with or destroy? You're right! You feel! You have the only real vision of the world. You love! No one else exists in the world except you, and those who can help you. Everyone else is nothing or else they're something to be destroyed. I'm your enemy now . . . right? I'm wrong. You are the children's father . . . but I'm no longer their mother. Every one of your yesses or nos is intended by you to re-shape the world after the image you have of it. They *are* my children! I am their mother! But because somehow I've become your enemy, I suddenly no longer qualify. Forget you're their mother, Grace. Walker has decided that you're no longer to perform that function. So the whole business is erased as if it never existed. I'm *not* in your head, Walker.

Neither are those kids. We are all flesh and blood and deserve to live . . . even unabstracted by what you think we ought to be in the general scheme of things. Even alien to it. I left you . . . and took the girls because you'd gone crazy. You're crazy now. This stupid ugly killing you've started will never do anything, for anybody. And you and all your people will be wiped out, you know that. And you'll have accomplished nothing. Do you want those two babies to be with you when you're killed so they can witness the death of a great man? So they can grow up and write articles for a magazine sponsored by the Walker Vessels Society?

WALKER. Which is still better than being freakish mulattoes in a world where your father is some evil black thing you can't remember. Look, I was going to wait until the fighting was over . . .
  [*Reflective*]
until we had won, before I took them. But something occurred to me for the first time, last night. It was the idea that we might not win. Somehow it only got through to me last night. I'd sort've taken it for granted . . . as a solved problem, that the fighting was the most academic of our problems, and that the real work would come necessarily after the fighting was done. But . . .

EASLEY. Things are not going as well for you as you figured.

WALKER. No. It will take a little longer, that's all. But this city will fall soon. We should be here within a week. You see, I could have waited until then. Then just marched in, at the head of the triumphant army, and seized the children as a matter of course. In fact I don't know why I didn't, except I did want to see you all in what you might call your natural habitats. I thought maybe I might be able to sneak in just as you and my ex-wife were making love, or just as you were lining the girls up against the wall to beat them or make them repeat after you, "Your daddy is a racist murderer." And then I thought I could murder both of you on the spot, and be completely justified.

GRACE. You've convinced yourself that you're rescuing the children, haven't you?

WALKER. Just as you convinced yourself you were rescuing them when you took them away from me.

EASLEY. She was!

WALKER. Now so am I.

GRACE. Yes
　　[*Wearily*]
I begin to get some of your thinking now. When you mentioned killing us. I'm sure you thought the whole thing up in quite heroic terms. How you'd come through the white lines, murder us, and *rescue* the girls. You probably went over that . . . or had it go through your head on that gray film, a thousand times until it was some kind of obligatory reality.
　　[WALKER *laughs*]

EASLEY. The kind of insane reality that brought about all the killing.

WALKER. Christ, the worst thing that ever happened to the West was the psychological novel . . . believe me.

EASLEY. When the Nazis were confronted with Freud, they claimed his work was of dubious value.

WALKER. Bravo!

GRACE. It's a wonder you *didn't* murder us!

WALKER.
[*Looking suddenly less amused*]
Oh . . . have I forfeited my opportunity?

EASLEY.
[*Startled reaction*]
You're not serious? What reason . . . what possible reason would there be for killing us? I mean I could readily conceive of your killing me, but the two of us, as some kind of psychological unit. I don't understand that. You said you didn't hate Grace.

GRACE.
[*To press* WALKER]
He's lying again, Brad. Really, most times he's not to be taken seriously. He was making a metaphor before . . . one of those ritual-drama metaphors . . .
[*Laughs, as does* BRAD]
You said it before . . . just to hear what's going on in his head. Really, he's not to be taken seriously.
[*She hesitates, and there is a silence*]
Unless there's some way you can kill him.

WALKER.

[*Laughs, then sobers, but begins to show the effects of the alcohol*]

Oh, Grace, Grace. Now you're trying to incite your husbean . . . which I swear is hardly Christian. I'm really surprised at you. But more so because you completely misunderstand me now . . . or maybe I'm not so surprised. I guess you never did know what was going on. That's why you left. You thought I betrayed you or something. Which really knocked me on my ass, you know? I was preaching hate the white man . . . get the white man off our backs . . . if necessary, kill the white man for our rights . . . whatever the hell that finally came to mean. And don't, now, for God's sake start thinking he's disillusioned, he's cynical, or any of the rest of these horseshit liberal definitions of the impossibility or romanticism of idealism. But those things I said . . . and would say now, pushed you away from me. I couldn't understand that.

GRACE. You couldn't understand it? What are you saying?

WALKER. No, I couldn't understand it. We'd been together a long time, before all that happened. What I said . . . what I thought I had to do . . . I knew you, if any white person in the world could, I knew you would understand. And then you didn't.

GRACE. You began to align yourself with the worst kind of racists and second-rate hack political thinkers.

WALKER. I've never aligned myself with anything or anyone I hadn't thought up first.

GRACE. You stopped telling me everything!

WALKER. I never stopped telling you I loved you . . . or that you were my wife!

GRACE.
    [*Almost broken*]
It wasn't enough, Walker. It wasn't enough.

WALKER. God, it should have been.

GRACE. Walker, you were preaching the murder of all white people. Walker, I was, am, white. What do you think was going through my mind every time you were at some rally or meeting whose sole purpose was to bring about the destruction of white people?

WALKER. Oh, goddamn it, Grace, are you so stupid? You were my wife . . . I loved you. You mean because I loved you and was married to you . . . had had children by you, I wasn't supposed to say the things I felt. I was crying out against three hundred years of oppression; not against individuals.

EASLEY. But it's individuals who are dying.

WALKER. It was individuals who were doing the oppressing. It was individuals who were being oppressed. The horror is that oppression is not a concept that can be specifically transferable. From the oppressed, down on the oppressor. To keep the horror where it belongs . . . on those people who we can speak of, even in this last part of the twentieth century, as evil.

EASLEY. You're so wrong about everything. So terribly, sickeningly wrong. What can you change? What do you hope to change? Do you think Negroes are better people than whites . . . that they can govern a society *better* than whites? That they'll be more judicious or more tolerant? Do you think they'll make fewer mistakes? I mean really, if the Western white man has proved one thing . . . it's the futility of modern society. So the have-not peoples become the haves. Even so, will that change the essential functions of the world? Will there be more love or beauty in the world . . . more knowledge . . . because of it?

WALKER. Probably. Probably there will be more . . . if more people have a chance to understand what it is. But that's not even the point. It comes down to baser human endeavor than any social-political thinking. What does it matter if there's more love or beauty? Who the fuck cares? Is that what the Western ofay thought while he was ruling . . . that his rule somehow brought more love and beauty into the world? Oh, he might have thought that concomitantly, while sipping a gin rickey and scratching his ass . . . but that was not ever the point. Not even on the Crusades. The point is that you had your chance, darling, now these other folks have theirs.
    [*Quietly*]
Now they have theirs.

EASLEY. God, what an ugly idea.

WALKER.

[*Head in hands*]

I know. I know.

[*His head is sagging, but he brings it up quickly. While it is down,* EASLEY *crosses* GRACE *with a significant look*]

But what else you got, champ? What else you got? I remember too much horseshit from the other side for you to make much sense. Too much horseshit. The cruelty of it, don't you understand, now? The complete ugly horseshit cruelty of it is that there doesn't have to be a change. It'll be up to individuals on that side, just as it was supposed to be up to individuals on this side. Ha! . . . Who failed! Just like you failed, Easley. Just like you failed.

EASLEY. Failed? What are you talking about?

WALKER.

[*Nodding*]

Well, what do you think? You never did anything concrete to avoid what's going on now. Your sick liberal lip service to whatever was the least filth. Your high aesthetic disapproval of the political. Letting the sick ghosts of the thirties strangle whatever chance we had.

EASLEY. What are you talking about?

WALKER. What we argued about so many times . . . befo' de wah.

EASLEY. And you see . . . what I predicted has happened. Now, in whatever cruel, and you said it, cruel political synapse you're taken with, or anyone else is taken with, with

sufficient power I, any individual, any person who thinks
of life as a purely anarchic relationship between man and
God . . . or man and his work . . . any consciousness
like that is destroyed . . . along with your *enemies*. And
you, for whatever right or freedom or sickening cause you
represent, kill me. Kill what does not follow.

WALKER. Perhaps you're right. But I have always found it
hard to be neutral when faced with ugliness. Especially an
ugliness that has worked all my life to twist me.

GRACE. And so you let it succeed!

WALKER. The aesthete came long after all the things that
really formed me. It was the easiest weight to shed. And
I couldn't be merely a journalist . . . a social critic. No
social protest . . . right is in the act! And the act itself has
some place in the world . . . it makes some place for itself.
Right? But you all accuse me, not understanding that what
you represent, you, my wife, all our old intellectual cut-
throats, was something that was going to die anyway. One
way or another. You'd been used too often, backed off from
reality too many times. Remember the time, remember that
time long time ago, in the old bar when you and Louie Rino
were arguing with me, and Louie said then that he hated
people who wanted to change the world. You remember
that?

EASLEY. I remember the fight.

WALKER. Yeah, well, I know I thought then that none of
you would write any poetry either. I knew that you had

moved too far away from the actual meanings of life . . .
into some lifeless cocoon of pretended intellectual and emo-
tional achievement, to really be able to see the world again.
What was Rino writing before he got killed? Tired ellip-
tical little descriptions of what he could see out the window.

EASLEY. And how did he die?

WALKER. An explosion in the school where he was teaching.
[*Nodding*]

EASLEY. One of your terrorists did it.

WALKER. Yeah, yeah.

EASLEY. He was supposed to be one of your closest friends.

WALKER. Yeah, yeah.

GRACE. Yeah, yeah, yeah, yeah.
[*With face still covered*]

WALKER. We called for a strike to show the government
we had all the white intellectuals backing us.
[*Nodding*]
Hah, and the only people who went out were those tired
political hacks. No one wanted to be intellectually com-
promised.

EASLEY. I didn't go either.
[*Hunches* GRACE, *starts to ease out of his chair*]
And it was an intellectual compromise. No one in their
right mind could have backed your program completely.

WALKER. No one but Negroes.

EASLEY. Well, then, they weren't in their right minds. You'd twisted them.

WALKER. The country twisted 'em.
　　[*Still nodding*]
The country had twisted them for so long.
　　[*Head almost touching his chest*]

EASLEY.
　　[*Taking very cautious step toward* WALKER, *still talking*]
The politics of self-pity.
　　[*Indicates to* GRACE *that she is to talk*]

WALKER.
　　[*Head down*]
Yeah. Yeah.

EASLEY. The politics of self-pity.

GRACE.
　　[*Raising her head slowly to watch, almost petrified*]
A murderous self-pity. An extraordinarily murderous self-pity.
　　[*There is another explosion close to the house. The lights go out for a few seconds. They come on, and* EASLEY *is trying to return to his seat, but* WALKER's *head is still on his chest*]

WALKER.
　　[*Mumbles*]
What'd they do, hit the lights? Goddamn lousy marksmen.
　　[EASLEY *starts again*]

Lousy marksmen . . . and none of 'em worth shit.

    [*Now, another close explosion. The lights go out again. They come on;* EASLEY *is standing almost halfway between the couch and* WALKER. WALKER's *head is still down on his chest.* EASLEY *crouches to move closer. The lights go out again*]

                                                            Black

[*More explosions*]

Act II

Explosions are heard before the curtain goes up. When curtain rises, room is still in darkness, but the explosion does throw some light. Figures are still as they were at the end of first act; light from explosions outlines them briefly.

WALKER. Shit.
[*Lights come up.* WALKER'S *head is still down, but he is nodding from side to side, cursing something very drunkenly.* EASLEY *stands very stiffly in the center of the room, waiting to take another step.* GRACE *sits very stiffly, breathing heavily, on the couch, trying to make some kind of conversation, but not succeeding.* WALKER *has his hand in his jacket pocket, on the gun*]

GRACE. It is self-pity, and some weird ambition, Walker.
[*Strained silence*]
But there's no reason . . . the girls should suffer. There's . . . no reason.
[EASLEY *takes a long stride, and is about to throw himself at* WALKER, *when there is another explosion, and the lights go out again, very briefly. When they come up,* EASLEY *is set to leap, but* WALKER'S *head comes abruptly up. He stares drunk-*

enly at EASLEY, *not moving his hand. For some awkward dura-
tion of time the two men stare at each other, in almost the
same way as they had at the beginning of the play. Then* GRACE
screams]

GRACE. Walker!

[WALKER *looks at her slightly, and* EASLEY *throws himself on
him. The chair falls backward and the two men roll on the
floor.* EASLEY *trying to choke* WALKER. WALKER *trying to get
the gun out of his pocket*]

GRACE. Walker! Walker!

[*Suddenly,* WALKER *shoves one hand in* EASLEY's *face, shooting him without taking the gun from his pocket.* EASLEY
*slumps backward, his face twisted, his mouth open and work-
ing.* WALKER *rolls back off* EASLEY, *pulling the gun from his
pocket. He props himself against the chair, staring at the man's
face*]

GRACE. Walker.

[*Her shouts have become whimpers, and she is moving stiffly
toward* EASLEY]

Walker. Walker.

EASLEY.

[*Mouth is still working . . . and he is managing to get a few
sounds, words, out*]

WALKER.

[*Still staring at him, pulling himself up on the chair*]

Shut up, you!

[*To* EASLEY]

You shut up. I don't want to hear anything else from you.
You just die, quietly. No more talk.

GRACE. Walker!

[*She is screaming again*]

Walker!

[*She rushes toward* EASLEY, *but* WALKER *catches her arm and pushes her away*]

You're an insane man. You hear me, Walker?

[*He is not looking at her, he is still staring down at* EASLEY]

Walker, you're an insane man.

[*She screams*]

You're an insane man.

[*She slumps to the couch, crying*]

An insane man . . .

WALKER. No profound statements, Easley. No horseshit like that. No elegance. You just die quietly and stupidly. Like niggers do. Like they are now.

[*Quieter*]

Like I will. The only thing I'll let you say is, "I only regret that I have but one life to lose for my country." You can say that.

[*Looks over at* GRACE]

Grace! Tell Bradford that he can say, "I only regret that I have but one life to lose for my country." You can say that, Easley, but that's all.

EASLEY.

[*Straining to talk*]

Ritual drama. Like I said, ritual drama . . .

[*He dies.*

WALKER *stands staring at him. The only sounds are an occasional explosion, and* GRACE's *heavy brittle weeping*]

WALKER. He could have said, "I only regret that I have but

one life to lose for my country." I would have let him say that . . . but no more. No more. There is no reason he should go out with any kind of dignity. I couldn't allow that.

GRACE. You're out of your mind.
[*Slow, matter-of-fact*]

WALKER. Meaning?

GRACE. You're out of your mind.

WALKER.
[*Wearily*]
Turn to another station.

GRACE. You're out of your mind.

WALKER. I said, turn to another station . . . will you? Another station! Out of my mind is not the point. You ought to know that.
[*Brooding*]
The way things are, being out of your mind is the only thing that qualifies you to stay alive. The only thing. Easley was in his right mind. Pitiful as he was. That's the reason he's dead.

GRACE. He's dead because you killed him.

WALKER. Yeah. He's dead because I killed him. Also, because he thought he ought to kill me.
[*Looking over at the dead man*]
You want me to cover him up?

GRACE. I don't want you to do anything, Walker . . . but leave here.

> [*Raising her voice*]

Will you do that for me . . . or do you want to kill me too?

WALKER. Are you being ironic? Huh?

> [*He grabs her arm, jerking her head up so she has to look at him*]

Do you think you're being ironic? Or do you want to kill me, too? . . .

> [*Shouting*]

You're mighty right I want to kill you. You're mighty god-damn right. Believe me, self-righteous little bitch, I want to kill you.

GRACE.

> [*Startled, but trying not to show it*]

The cause demands it, huh? The cause demands it.

WALKER. Yeah, the cause demands it.

GRACE.

> [*She gets up and goes to* EASLEY, *kneeling beside the body*]

The cause demands it, Brad. That's why Walker shot you . . . because the cause demands it.

> [*Her head droops but she doesn't cry. She sits on her knees, holding the dead man's hand*]

I guess the point is that now when you take the children I'll be alone.

> [*She looks up at* WALKER]

I guess that's the point, now. Is that the point, Walker? Me being alone . . . as you have been now for so long?

I'll bet that's the point, huh? I'll bet you came here to do exactly what you did . . . kill Brad, then take the kids, and leave me alone . . . to suffocate in the stink of my memories.

[*She is trying not to cry*]

Just like I did to you. I'm sure that's the point. Right?

[*She leaps up suddenly at* WALKER]

You scum! You murdering scum.

[*They grapple for a second, then* WALKER *slaps her to the floor. She kneels a little way off from* EASLEY'S *body*]

WALKER.   Yeh, Grace. That's the point. For sure, that's the point.

GRACE. You were going to kill Brad, from the first. You knew that before you even got here.

WALKER. I'd thought about it.

GRACE.

[*Weeping, but then she stops and is quiet for a minute*]

So what's supposed to happen then . . . I mean after you take the kids and leave me here alone? Huh? I know you've thought about that, too.

WALKER. I have. But you know what'll happen much better than I do. But maybe you don't. What do you think happened to me when you left? Did you ever think about that? You must have.

GRACE. You had your cause, friend. Your cause, remember. And thousands of people following you, hoping that shit you preached was right. I pitied you.

WALKER. I know that. It took me awhile, but then I finally understood that you did pity me. And that you were somewhere, going through whatever mediocre routine you and Easley called your lives . . . pitying me. I figured that, finally, you weren't really even shocked by what was happening . . . what had happened. You were so secure in the knowledge that you were good, and compassionate . . . and right, that most of all . . . you were certain, my God, so certain . . . emotionally and intellectually, that you were right, until the only idea you had about me was to pity me.

[*He wheels around to face her squarely*]

God, that pissed me off. You don't really know how furious that made me. You and that closet queen, respected, weak-as-water intellectual, pitying me. God. God!

[*Forcing the humor*]

Miss Easley, honey, I could have killed both of you every night of my life.

GRACE. Will you kill me now if I say right here that I still pity you?

WALKER.

[*A breathless half-broken little laugh*]

No. No, I won't kill you.

GRACE. Well, I pity you, Walker. I really do.

WALKER. Only until you start pitying yourself.

GRACE. I wish I could call you something that would hurt you.

WALKER. So do I.

GRACE.
[*Wearily*]
Nigger.

WALKER. So do I.
[*Looks at his watch*]
I've got to go soon.

GRACE. You're still taking the girls.
[*She is starting to push herself up from the floor.*

WALKER *stares at her, then quickly over his shoulder at the stairway. He puts his hand in the pocket where the gun is, then he shakes his head slowly*]

GRACE.
[*Not seeing this gesture*]
You're still taking the children?
[WALKER *shakes his head slowly. An explosion shakes the house a little*]

GRACE. Walker. Walker.
[*She staggers to her feet, shaking with the next explosion*]
Walker? You shook your head?
[WALKER *stands very stiffly looking at the floor.*

GRACE *starts to come to him, and the next explosion hits very close or actually hits the house. Beams come down; some of the furniture is thrown around.* GRACE *falls to the floor.* WALKER *is toppled backward. A beam hits* GRACE *across the chest. Debris falls on* WALKER. *There are more explosions, and then silence*]

GRACE. Walker! Walker!
> [*She is hurt very badly and is barely able to move the debris that is covering her*]

Walker! The girls! Walker! Catherine! Elizabeth! Walker, the girls!
> [WALKER *finally starts to move. He is also hurt badly, but he is able to move much more freely than* GRACE. *He starts to clear away the debris and make his way to his knees*]

GRACE. Walker?

WALKER. Yeah? Grace?

GRACE. Walker, the children . . . the girls . . . see about the girls.
> [*She is barely able to raise one of her arms*]

The girls, Walker, see about them.

WALKER.
> [*He is finally able to crawl over to* GRACE, *and pushes himself unsteadily up on his hands*]

You're hurt pretty badly? Can you move?

GRACE. The girls, Walker, see about the girls.

WALKER. Can you move?

GRACE. The girls, Walker . . .
> [*She is losing strength*]

Our children!

WALKER.
> [*He is silent for a while*]

They're dead, Grace. Catherine and Elizabeth are dead.
> [*He starts up stairs as if to verify his statement. Stops, midway, shakes his head; retreats*]

GRACE.
> [*Looking up at him frantically, but she is dying*]

Dead? Dead?
> [*She starts to weep and shake her head*]

Dead?
> [*Then she stops suddenly, tightening her face*]

How . . . how do you know, Walker? How do you know they're dead?
> [WALKER's *head is drooping slightly*]

How do you know they're dead, Walker? How do you . . .
> [*Her eyes try to continue what she is saying, but she slumps, and dies in a short choking spasm.*
>
> WALKER *looks to see that she is dead, then resumes his efforts to get up. He looks at his watch. Listens to see if it is running. Wipes his face. Pushes the floor to get up. Another explosion sounds very close and he crouches quickly, covering his head. Another explosion. He pushes himself up, brushing sloppily at his clothes. He looks at his watch again, then starts to drag himself toward the door*]

They're dead, Grace!
> [*He is almost shouting*]

They're dead.
> [*He leaves, stumbling unsteadily through the door. He is now the old man at the beginning of the play. There are more explosions. Another one very close to the house. A sudden aggravated silence, and then there is a child heard crying and screaming as loud as it can. More explosions*]

Black

[*More explosions, after curtain for some time*]

The children are dead / socially neither parent or peers will except the children – hatred / social injustice / non rea